GARLAND

Flowers of Spirit

Sam Burcher

GARLAND

Published by Sam Burcher © 2013

ISBN: 978 0957579309

Distributed by Pine Cone, London.
Printed by Berforts, Oxford.

Sam Burcher was born in Westminster. She was educated at the Henrietta Barnett School in Hampstead Garden Suburb, the Camberwell School of Arts and Crafts, and has an MSc. from the London South Bank University.

She has co-authored several key reports on green energies, food futures and health. She works with a number of campaign and cross-party parliamentary groups.

Sam is a member of the London Press Club and writes for a number of science and environment journals as well as a regular column for *Caduceus* magazine

Garland is her first collection of poems, lyrics and prose-sequences in the form of very short stories.

She lives in London with her partner Andy.

Introduction by Nick Papadimitriou

I first met Sam Burcher at the October Gallery in Bloomsbury in the winter of 2001. We were both beginning our first day as researchers with a science institute. I immediately found in her a kindred spirit: both of us were motivated by a strong sense of social and environmental justice; both of us longed to become writers.

It was in front of the smoky open fire in her living room that Sam first chose to reveal her considerable talent for playing guitar and lyric writing. To this day I retain the memory of a song replete with curious trilling and complex chord changes. I was utterly charmed.

Over the next few months we set to, writing reports and essays which were disseminated throughout the world of environmental research via magazines, conferences, governmental reports and the internet. However, we continued to write for ourselves, and I went on to produce several books and radio series concerned specifically with topography and place.

When Sam sent me her draft of this book I was seized with anticipation. How had her more personal writings developed since 2001? *Garland* brings to fruition everything she has worked for these past twelve years. This collection comprises a wide variety of highly personal and striking takes on life. As well as the compellingly detailed travel pieces, written during various visits to the Mediterranean, Sam focuses on her London life, effectively defamiliarising what, in the hands of lesser writers, would be the most mundane conditions.

Elsewhere in the collection, Sam dips into the storehouse of mythology, drawing half-familiar elements from the ancient world into the light of the modern era. Several poems are concerned with the vagaries of life: health problems, relationships and the perils of political and environmental activism. These provide Sam with themes which rouse her latent social passion. *Garland* is not always an easy ride, but what you find here will resonate with you months and years later.

Nick P.
London, April, 2013.

Contents

LONDON

LIFE AND DEATH

MUSIC

NATURE AND PSYCHE

GROWTH

PLACE

Random (Light and Matter)

Elements

SONGS: LYRICS OF CHANGE AND INTEGRATION

London

FLOWERS OF SPIRIT

I arrive here,
alive with spirit breath.
I hold myself on the inside,
and work my energy
downward, outward and
upward –
All poets have flowers in their chests.

LONDON MORNING

Guess what collided with a 4x4, and lost?
A butterfly, of course.
She picked it up by damaged wings,
and put in on a flower again.

The earth crackles underfoot.
She goes deeper underground,
where the world, his wife, and her children
crowd onto the Stratford train.

She travels alone.

Passed Westminster Palace into the park.
A homeless man is picking his teeth
after eating a donated sandwich.
Her open-toe sandles soak up the morning dew.

'Meet me by the Tate pontoon,' he'd said.

She walks sedately by the children chasing pigeons,
and watches daytime drinkers
swigging beer in Victoria Tower gardens.
It's not even eleven in the morning.

She's early, so time to watch the river
and smell the nicotine spike the blood
of cigarette smokers sitting beside her.
She's quit and learnt to breathe instead.

LOSING MIND

I hear the voices in my head
of friends and enemies.
I listen to the city's drone
interfering with my dreams.

I hear the cries for help
rising from suburban lawns.
I watch the shadow people
cough and spit on city streets,

betraying their own connections,
betraying their own desires,
taking wrong directions,
losing vision, losing mind.

The sea is at the land's edge,
the city's heart a paving stone.
Here until I'm no longer here,
I'll stay until I'm gone.

ADVERSARY EYES

Two artists saved my life today
when pain and grief had seized me
after meeting by chance an old adversary-friend,
who had not the wit to remember my name
and I not the wit to forget.
We stared into the window pane
of Daunt Books on Belsize Lane.
I was looking at a biography of
Sybil Bedford, or Mrs Aldous Huxley.
We talked, '*Did you ever give up smoking?*'
she drawled. And I saw through her cynicism,
as she narrowed her eyes like a cold reptile
on a dark night sitting beside a Bedouin fire,
telling stories of a sacred kind.

The familiar street suddenly so fearful,
people and cars move out of time,
traffic lights are martians under blackening skies.
The universe is suspended and for a moment
I die, and see a raindrop on my shore,
a violet-blue horizon blowing through
my kinder eyes, stopping a tear or two.
Inside, my spirit splutters for eternal breath;
nervous twitching, muscles flexing, heart rate racing.
I pretend I read the paper to the outside world,
turning until I come upon two paintings on the page.
I fix on a sunset vision of Margate,
my calm restored and thirsty spirit slaked,
made whole by J.M.W. Turner and William Blake.

STILL

I thought that abstinence would help me cope with London life: no cigarettes, no alcohol, no chocolates, and still I feel fit for nothing. The taste of fuel is on my tongue, the residue of compressed ancient sunlight in my lungs.

I am somewhere in between the sorrow and the pain, neither fighting nor submitting, just witnessing and writing. Writing in the place where my tears move. And I am filled with grace.

Culture? We are all just products of culture, man-made minds producing paradigms. Where are the wilds of pollen and panthers?

We still run guns to bring down our children. We still spray chemicals to kill the bees. We still drop bombs on innocent towns and still chop down the trees.

I keep my fear and vanity close to me in a case with a mirror, so I can check I'm still here.

BELINDA'S SONG

Orange hairdye,
yellow Renault,
beaded curtains,
red bordello,
leopard-skin wallpaper,
thigh high boots,
she sold her house
to Peter O'Toole.
She flies her freedom flag high,
she flies her freedom flag
high, high, high.

She's got demons,
mirrored ceilings,
smokes her reefers
every evening.
Mick Jones her favourite,
she's playing
London Calling,
on her stereo.
She flies her freedom flag high,
she flies her freedom flag,
high, high, high.

She's an old soul
who went new wave,
got a toyboy,
half her own age.
Fills her garage
full of vintage
clothes for charity,
War on Want.
She flies her freedom flag high,
she flies her freedom flag,
high, high, high.

She's got knowledge,
not from college,
learnt her lessons,
on the music scene.
Seduced my brother
under cover,
now she's a teacher
in Palmers Green.
She flies her freedom flag high,
she flies her freedom flag,
high, high, high.

FRANKINCENSE AND SALT

They burned your body
on the beach,
but your big heart wouldn't burn,
so they wrapped it in a manuscript
tempered with frankincense and salt.

I return to the graveside
where you first met her
finding solace in the presence
of the long since departed,
under watchful gothic spires,
in the late November rain.

I shelter in old St Pancras Church,
putting my last few coins
into the slot
to buy a postcard
and light a candle,

I pray,
not that the rain will stop,
but for more Love in this world.

You might think that we're all poets now,
but it's still a struggle
between the haves and the have-nots.

And deep within, I know
the divine fire can never be doused.
Our skies will never be silent,
we have filled them with *sotto voce* clouds.

LIFE AND DEATH

LAMENT

My mother
lost her brother
to a sniper in World War II
and a sister to diphtheria.
When she was 16,
my mother's father died
of a brain hemorrhage
brought on by shell shock and the gas
in the trenches of World War I.
Nine months before I was born
my mother's mother died.
My father made
no allowances for my mother's grief.
His own was neatly packed
into a school trunk and sent away
to boarding school after
his mother died giving birth to twins
when he was four.
A deep black depression
has stalked my soul.
My parents' suppressed tears
has left me a legacy.
With this lament,
my life begins.

GONE A WEEK

You've only been gone a week
and my tears are still unspent.
I'm hurt by the things that you said,
so I gave all your clothes away.

Do you wish that we'd never met,
or found pleasure in the things we did?
Washing all that messy linen in public.
Been better off if we'd hid!

You know all I wanted was to sing,
but you slapped me down for that dream.
Disappearing round corners, gone for hours
with more than just sweets in your bag.

Do you wish that we'd slowed right down,
or tried to bring our feelings to ground,
breaking into our own house,
when we lost the keys that we'd found?

We could have been clinging to each other,
instead of tearing precious spirits apart,
and twisting up our bitter sweet chances.
You've only been gone a week.

WOMAN IN THE WINDOW

The woman in the window
has packed up his clothes
and loaded them into the car,
and taken them away.

Now she weeds the path,
and prunes the privet.
She sweeps up the dead leaves,
as he whispers his goodbye.

A piano song carries on the wind
to the sound of distant laughter.
He's gone. She stays.

SUICIDAL WIVES

Each day will see her beauty
made anew,
but her love has turned to blue.
Her flowing hair and freckled face
cannot conceal the soulless place
where love has turned to blue.

This shiny idyll sparkling deep,
should surely be enough to keep
her a captive of his life,
but he has made her his wife,
and turned her love to blue.

REMEMBER YOU DIE (MOMENTO MORI)

Live each day
just to stay
under this sweet sun,
rich with love for everything
and everyone.

To stay alive,
occupy your life
in the feeling present,
aligned with your conditions
and your purpose.

Mindful of conscience,
mindful of the whole,

and the power in the pieces.

ME

This is me:
I am emerging,
not an emergency
or a stretcher case baby.
Don't call the paramedics.
This is me, emerging
here, now.
No need to dial 999,
'Someone stop him, he's gone mad,
our lad's gone bad.'

Now it's over:
this is my emergence,
not my emergency.
I am calm. Now
the personal crisis is accepted,
it is safe for me to
shine.

WITNESS

I left my body
far behind
during the time of
your violence.

> My leaking soul
> shot towards
> the ceiling, and
> evaporated.

My heart
fell out of my chest,
my nerves and brain
exploded.

> My spinal column
> froze, my spirit
> cried out in pain,
> my tears to no avail.

My petitions could not
change
the cycles of your
rage.

LITTLE TYGER

You, not yet tall
as a late March daffodil,
grab my hands
with your softly padded paws
and tensile claws.

Little Tyger, you remind me
of your smallness and my size.
I rub your nose
with my finger, a gesture,
and suddenly, I am mother,
transmitting love
through my hands
to your fur.

You purr,
so I change tack
to keep you amused.
My feet without shoes
rub your tummy,
you push on my soles,
and chew a little on my toes.

I think of my parents,
and the child I never had.
I think of my lover,
and how we felt,
the sensuality,
the purity,
and then I expand.

I think of life and death
all in this moment.
How dare I think of death
when fat purple figs ripen on the branches
and apples bend the golden boughs?

Little Tyger, sweet paws,
the softness of you at my feet
completing love's connection.

I look to the sky –
death is the final outcome,
and life I simplify.

ONCOLOGY WARD

I'm in bed, in the Women's Hospital in Soho Square. The nurses are whispering. One of them mentions cancer and I think I'm hallucinating.

She sits on the bed and breaks the news. 'Well, the condition you have is cancerous, but the doctors haven't told you yet.' I'm trapped in blindingly white sheets and can't take this in without a pen.

Now I'm hazy and just out of intensive care. I'm being transferred to Charing Cross Hospital where they deal with this sort of 'one in a million' thing. This state of the art hospital towering over Fulham Palace Road is shockingly modern. I'm given a room of my own on ward Nine West with views to die for.

He sends a card, it's a transparent pink flower and some-one sticks it to the gloriously wide window, letting the light pass through the petals. He has written, 'You turn me on' in marker pen along the edge. It makes me happy that he is thinking about me in such a positive way.

I am 21 and have got the key to the oncology ward. The bouquets start to arrive. I work in the music industry and they have expense accounts. Pretty soon I am drowning in a sea of calla lilies and things become revealed to me as if I were a character in a Diego Rivera painting; someone central, someone who is needed. I am humbled.

He visits every day with his long denim legs and we lie top to tail like two sardines on my bed. He is devoted to me and pleasures me a little in the private bathroom when all my life-support tubes have been taken out. The line in my jugular is the hardest to bear.

My mother comes every day, her long hair swinging into action with the nurses and the other patients. And so does Wendy, with her teddy bear get well cards and infectious giggle.

My father comes once in the three months of treatment. He is hard working. I see him slip into the room, just after I've received my first dose of intravenous chemotherapy and it seems as if I'm holding the whole world and the oceans in my hands.

LUMBAR PUNCTURE

Every Wednesday
the nurse comes
to take fluid
from my spinal cord.

He tugs and pulls
with his needle
but *I* mustn't move a millimetre
or even flinch:

I call it a hollow invasion.

He mixes my life energy
with a drug and injects
it all back into my spine.
A necessary trauma to heal tumours.

Afterwards I lay flat for twenty four hours.
One day closer to life.

MUSIC

SINGER'S EGO

The singer's ego's like no other,
transcending all space and time,
aligns to no-one, is lonely,
spectacularly foolhardy and kind.

This singer's ego had to hide
in hedgerows and behind blinds,
or sometimes in a garden shed,
my words left unsung and unsaid.

The singer's ego swims in
waves of sound way above the ground,
on dulcet wings of birds that fly,
the singer's ego, my oh my!

GAME OF LIFE

I found the Ace of Spades
in the street,
but I swapped my aces
for twos in life's
game of Pontoon.
Oh, silly fool!

The crows are calling me
back to my song
to finish what I started.

88 Keys

I delete romance
from my inbox.
I disconnect
the internet,
turn off the television
and switch on the radio.
I'm not ready yet
to compare the fantasy
to reality.

I listen to the sound
of your fingers
on the keys,
Debussy blue.

Images tumbling,
as your notes review
the two tone questions
you asked in wandering woods.
Among the trees and birds
where green turns gold,
you pause and look around,
like a wounded stag about to go down.

As the light shades towards the night,
you cannot forget
your glittering instrument.

Your shining soul
is seeking happiness
amidst these senseless wars.
Pennies shaping cheap pleasures.

No chains can bind
your melodic footsteps
that skip
over the base pairs
that stitch
the parallel chords
that chime
together.

You have beaten time,

your fingers
        on the keys
                playing *Clair de Lune.*

THE MUSES BLUES

I stand here watching you play.
I expand here as you play your guitar,
shocked by your purity,
your discipline, your sound.

The muses are waiting in your shadow,
always around you like friends.
I almost remember, but soon I forget,
and drown in the sound of your set.

You stand there under the stage lights,
your fingers so graceful and long.
The muses are gathering round you,
willing you on to your song.

The muses are always in your orbit,
or lingering about in the crowd.
I almost remember my own sweet song,
then forget why I'm around.

Come back to me my muses,
you've been gone for far too long.
Come back to me my muses,
return to me my own sweet song.

DEAR SERGE

I thought you died in 1975 changing a lightbulb,
my dear Gainsbourg, my dear Serge.

But all the while the melody was waiting for you –
long blue shadows on the wall.

I watch helplessly as you bring
the stars into the room as you sing.

The stars shine on your every word,
my dear Gainsbourg, my dear Serge.

EVERYTHING COMES IN WAVES...

Structures dissolve into chaos
then reconfigure
into higher orders of complexity.
And as the tones get higher
so does the frequency:
increasing complexity,
increasing consciousness.

In chaos,
no coherent forms are seen
just chaos and re-integration
on ever-changing seas of vibration.
The wave atoms of sound oscillate
and going orbital inside their shells,
become observable phenomena.

NATURE AND PSYCHE

SHUTTERED BREEZE 1

My fluid mind
flows round trees
in closed woods,
on shuttered breeze.

I smooth blankets
over shattered sheets
on glass bed,
and then cry

my albumin tears
tumble down cheeks
exposed and naked
under moon tide.

My net cast
catches shimmering fish
left gasping under
red shrinking skies.

Marooned and ashore
my fish-eyed quarry
stare surprised at
death's awesome divide.

Shuttered Breeze 2

My fluid mind flows round trees
in closed woods on shuttered breeze.

I ride horseback on fractal pathways,
                    drawing the reins towards
          my centre,

high above ditches and dog walkers,
                    sensing the dangers of life.

Gravity shifts, I lean back and canter down
          to
               the
                    doorway.

THE PARADOX TREE

Now I see the bows and arrows,
the catapults and vital purpose,
the myriad possibilities.

Now the leaves have fallen,
revealing the curvatures and tangled complexities
of the paradox tree.

Its nature is to bend
and bring buds and branches
into the service of animals and humanity.
A fine line between use and service,
love and peace, war and hate.
Between giving up and sacrifice.
Between nest and shelter.

Dendrite branches make mathematical patterns,
coaxing blue from pale winter skies. They shield
satellite-marked houses from each other's sight,
blind eyes with lances and separate with fences.

Now gather in baskets the nodes of divine life,
and burn your weapons around campfires,
singing and strumming guitars, drumming out unity.

I see the hardening lignen,
the pulsating sap within,
the parts dividing and the wholeness,
in stages: a signpost, a railway sleeper,
a vision song, a messenger with open arms.

THE NUMINOSUM

This is the woodsmoke moment;
the sacred space between the past,
and the ever present now,
where sunlight streams on blades of grass,
and new shoots strive to meet the sky.

This planet is alive.

The Earth pulsates and hums.
I am magnetically charged with life.
A soil sister suspended on my path.
The air is heavy and sweet
with natural successions.

Grounded and complete,
I'm far away from city street,
shrouded by hills and oak-lined ridge,
skeletal stands on winter's meagre skyline.

Starlings murmur as they congregate,
the swirling flocks resonate.
Throwing shapes
they land in trees,
substitutes for fallen leaves.

In this moment there is connection,
and I evoke the numinosum.

THE BIRD

I see the bird through my window.
It sits in silence
in the snow.

My fear expands instead of my joy:
fear of the snow and of winter
and the terrifyingly white sky.

Is the bird a vulture
come to peck out the eyes of summer?
Or an owl in silent calculation?
I know his long grey feathers,
but cannot name his type.

The bird just sits and stares.

I run with my tears to the garden
to lay out an offering,
hands full of bread and rice and seed.
The bird does not eat.

Baby Blackbird

An ant runs up my leg,
wood pigeons steal cherries
from the cherry tree.
I settle down
and feel a sharpness
poking through the blanket,
which was laid over the grass.

I pull back the shroud,
and there the little bird lies,
its beak had pierced the fabric
and drilled into my flesh.

It's June, and baby birds die.
No rescue.

His beak will never yellow,
nor will he ever sing
sweet overtones,
or eat earthworms and hawthorn berries,
or make sharp contrast against
white winter's snow.

The baby blackbird
lies among windfall apples,
dropped before they have even ripened,
like you, my love.

Butterfly

I, butterfly
never want to
be pinned, trapped
or captured.

I, papillion
never want to
die, twirling in
a wordless sky.

I, schmetterling
feel my spirit light,
let me
fly, fly, fly.

Butterflies

I am high,
living and re-living the light.
I cry
as butterflies fight,
a meadow brown and cabbage white,
to possess my wild
garden of earthly delight.

I Am

I am
the butterfly,
flying through
the hurricane,
floating
over earthquakes,
dancing in the void again.

I am
the never
forgotton one,
chasing rainbows,
beyond tornadoes,
streaming
on particles
of light.

I am
at the crossroads,
accepting knowledge
and desire,
in fearless moments,
moving on
with what I know.

HER HAT

Her hat is swathed in sunlight molecules.
She hides her eyes beneath its brim,
peering through pin-prick perforations
as the prismatic colours stream in.

The holes in her hat trap
tiny rainbow circles that overlap
with subatomic particles of light.
Neutrinos dance on golden rays, and weave
patterns in waves of love
alive in the sunshine.

The spectrum radiates more light
than she has ever seen before,
blazing through five dimensions,
accelerating and raising humanity's
evolutionary vibrations;
spiralling up with the angels towards Heaven –
Our final destination?

Here on Earth,
flowers are burning in violet light;
tulips shine in beer glass gardens
on stems so green
they make her think
of noisy ring-necked parakeets
patrolling English parks,
stripping bark off defenceless trees,
and breaking the wires
on her garden bird feeders.

The glass bird in her mind shatters.
Steel-blue feathers
and rainbow glints descend into her eye:
pink, green, yellow, orange-red and indigo;
electromagnetic protons
pulsating energy from trembling skies.

THE GARDEN

There are grass marks on my skin. The garden connects me to my senses in safety. Where do I begin? A frog has landed on my cushion and a butterfly in my ear. The frog is yellow, green and black. One gold lined eye watches me, his other eye is shy and winks a wicked wink. Perhaps he's a wicked prince looking to grab a kiss with his four short fingers and one long thumb. His throat is a pink speckled stone.

All around us apples are decaying on the ground. Wasps patrol the rotten fruit and I could easily put my bare feet down and be stung. In my green garden chives and chicory thrive, oregano bolts and brambles writhe.

I become the humming of bees and the breeze stirring the sun-sucked grass. An old fashioned sash splutters and rushes up as someone opens a window.

Bees and hoverflies are friends of mine, and deep down in my garden no pesticides I ply, despite the snails, slugs and green fly. I lie supine and think of you in your wood-land willow coffin as you turn your skull-face to me, and whisper: *'Terra, protect the Earth.'*

In the garden, my ash, apples, and raspberry canes all glow a different green under the Harvest Moon. September has come too quickly.

THE FULL MOON

The full moon fills my chest
until moonfluence pours from my eyes,
and leaches from my breasts.
I am oozing with its light waves.

My pilgrim gaze follows the
incandescent trail laid out before me
until my eyes and the moonrise are one.

Our moon could be earth's cast off mantle,
pulling on the tides,
and slowing moving mountains.

This is the special time
when the moon shares its blood filled nights
and rice paper days with the sun.
But this will/change. And our days will become longer.
    Soon

So until the moon tires of Earth's spin
and drifts away,
my footsteps follow the moon.

ANATOMICAL SHADOW

My pen rolls down the pages of the open book, which is
lying on the exposed white sheet, the duvet thrown back to
air in the morning sunshine. The shadow of the window
blind, spread across the bed, looks like a giant ribcage,
a mapping of the human sternum by slender wooden slats.

Now why did I think that? No, this shadow looks more
like sand waves rippling across some remembered shore.
My skin is striped with bands of black on golden flesh.
The pillows rest abandoned against the headboard, half in
shadow half in light.

GROWTH

THE DOORS

The doors slam.
Have I offended you again?
I feel guilty.
I let you down.

The doors slam
on this prison called life,
and I'm locked in.
I feel you reaching out to me
on the fringes
of my racial memory.

What do I want?
That's the million dollar question.
I still don't know.
I'm angry, afraid.

Closing my eyes, I see
a crowd looking in at me,
a circle of friendly faces –
my guides
on the threshold of my consciousness.

WHAT IF?

What if we were only ever judged for our greatness,
and all that greatness wasn't wrong? (Don't get me wrong,
you're great, but it's this song I'm chasing:-)

What if when we become gods of our own reality; when
we make the right choices, we become sweet beings?

What if we lifted the veils, believing with our own eyes
in the moment that we know that we know (not how
we know) we are one, and we are not alone?

The key to higher love is opening up, acceptance,
transformation – painful and exciting. The power of
letting go, shedding skin, letting light in, stopping the
sound of self-deprecation.

I have been thinking about it all along. I am a lonely
island on this planet, but we are all islands connected
underwater, so here goes...

You will know what I mean when you receive the
energy of love without judgment. I am a sea change of
consciousness, getting lighter in my sleep and in my
waking dreams.

We are all water drops of consciousness. More powerful
than any religion or judgment. A new reality.

BEYOND

I am beyond the beat,
beyond that and this
fake reality.

I taste the full fat
milky grace of stars
and shower bells of love
over my hungry ego.

My duality is changing,
hemispheres shifting.
I am learning my emotions,
going back into my fragmented soul
and integrating with awareness.

I call on the power within
to expand my energy
into a new vibration,
a higher frequency.

Drawing on divinity,
a god-self hologram greets me –
my entelechy, my eternal soul sister.
there is no wall between us.

THE WALL

All I could hear
was the voice saying to me,
*'Your fear is a wall
you must overcome
and ultimately bring down.*

*To tear down this wall
is your calling;
to challenge the fear
instilled in you by others,
and not to let terror
overwhelm you, no matter
how small you feel.*

*This wall was sent to test you,
but you must prevail
to scale it
and break it down
brick by brick,
and rebuild your house.'*

THE RULES

They say that people love people
who break the rules.
I was too cool for school,
but have mellowed on the vine
of my rebellion.

And those who disapproved of me then
find my past behaviour
acceptable now.

But still sometimes,
who I am
is disdained
just the same.

When will I fit into my own time?

Back then, my sparks kept igniting,
shaking desks in stifled classrooms.
My witty missiles kept launching,
guided by the laughter rocking my brain,
flying on the tailcoats of my self-appointed fame.

THE VINE

Let the sun shine through
a glass of red wine,
adding drops of light
three at a time
to make a tincture.

And then drink it.

Take in love from the red grape vine
straight to your heart's centre,
in grateful appreciation
of the sun's warmth,
and the wind-blown orbs.

I am amazed by my growth
and my movement.
I have laboured long,
and the fruits are in my favour.

THE ECSTASY

Don't take the crystals, you said,
so I exploded two on my tongue
for good measure.

Now this, she said.
I took two great pulls on her spliff,
and then hit the wall:

We are old friends my ego and I.
Sometimes, when I get high,
it likes to terrorize me.

While everyone is drinking and laughing
outside in the sunshine,
I'm locked in the bathroom;
overbreathing and staring at the mirror,
asking myself:

Who am I?
I don't want to die!

I enter another room, another tomb,
and sit cross-legged on the floor.

Finally,
I connect to my body,
and taking responsibility for myself,
I release the victim mentality.

Then hear the others coming to find me.

PLACES

HAMPSTEAD HEATH

The moorhens ignore us, but the ducks are making ever widening trails through the algae-covered ponds, and waggle out to greet us, looking for crumbs to eat.

They race back in as soon as a young Alsatian crashes into their territory, drinking thirstily, then thrashing the water like a madwoman doing her washing.

The oxygen rich woods reek of weed and Calvin Klein aftershave. Boys in blue jeans are emerging from the bushes, inexorably drawn to outdoor pleasures.

GLASTONBURY FESTIVAL

You pinned me to the floor
and gave me what for.

Our spirits soared above
the tent as we made love.

We shone in bliss,
you kissed my soul, my lips.

I blessed you once or twice,
and revelled in your blue skies.

Much later, wrapped in silver sheets,
We warmed our muddy hands and feet.

But after all that poison rain,
I never saw your blue sky again.

ROAD PROTEST

We are up on God's green hill, Saving Solsbury! It's my first night in a protest camp. And I wonder what I'm doing here. My cold feet feel as if they might turn to stone and crumble in the night.

But the day comes whole and new and the camp is getting organized. There's a fire to be mended, wood to be gathered and sacks full of food from the locals to be sorted. And there's coltsfoot to smoke and liquorish to chew. It's the end of June in Somerset and it's glorious.

After breakfast there's a strategy meeting to discuss pixies putting sugar in the fuel tanks of diggers. Then there are banners and faces to be painted. Later, I lead the candlelight vigil into the woods. Chatting up the yellow jacketed Group 4 security guards, we gain a defector.

I go to Bath and meet a programmer with a room full of computers and use a horoscope package to make charts for the tree-dwellers. But back on Solsbury, Group 4 thugs are throwing punches as we try to stop the diggers. I scamper back to camp, having learned to avoid violence. Some of the protesters return to the fire with bloody heads and torn sweaters.

I'll never forget Rob's voice, a distillate of hedgerows and didgeridoos. He named me "Cherub" to protect my anonymity, although Phoenix called me "SnogaSex" later, back in London, I don't know why.

Rob had a room above an abandoned stable where he made a shrine to nature on a millstone and worried about the world. 'Always leave a place better than you found it' he said.

We rowed with no rollocks to Bradford upon Avon to get more supplies – sleeping bags, boots and the like – pulling the boat over rocky weirs. 'Bollocks no rollocks!' we joked. And Rob ate his seed off his palm; nothing was wasted.

The woman from the Daily Mail slept in a yurt for a couple of nights. But the rest of us slept together in the communal bender. I didn't think I could sleep in the same space with so many other people, but it was bliss.

I meandered within the force-field of Solsbury Hill and the surrounding water meadows. I consulted the hedge sparrows about the new road. They said they wanted peace and fewer roads and less traffic. But the by-pass got built anyway. The woods were devastated.

DENIAL

'*Write to me*', you begged,
at the dance
in the Scout hut
in Digbeth.

I never did, because
I was in denial
of the words I needed.

CRETE

When the lilac has brindled
and lost its scent,
I shall be gone
across the phosphorescent seas,
bound for Crete
in search of my heroes,
the mythic men who haunt my dreams,

seeking out the ancient languages
spoken by the Greeks and the old Myceneans.
I'll mingle with the Minoans in temples at Knossos,
and try to decipher archaic symbols,
scored on stone tablets in Linear A and B.

Then overland to Stavros
where Anthony Quinn danced
Zorba's dance across the sand
of a horseshoe shaped bay.

I'll keep on searching
for what I may fail to find.
Until then, I bide my time
with birds and pollinating insects
in lilac scented gardens.

THE GHOST

This place got to me as soon as I arrived.
I sat down at the airport and cried,
then caught a yellow school bus that took me
to Panajachel from Guatemala city.
I sat beside ancient Lake Atitlan
and saw the shadows of that brave clan
which chose not to surrender, but to drown,
when the Conquistadors came to town.
Above the surface, sinewy arms
struck wildly at waters before sinking down.
Alone in my hotel room that night,
I was awakened by a strange sight:

An Indian woman stands silent by my bed,
the door locked firmly from inside.
She stares at me, our eyes meet.
I freeze in fear and pray for sleep.
Next morning, my bedside glass is smashed,
I run to check the door is still latched.
The nonchalent hotel owner is unperturbed.
'A ghost haunts your floor,' he murmured.
I tell my story all next day,
'You didn't speak to her?' they say.
'She would have taken you to the underworld.'
Somehow, I knew and understood.

ERICE

This is where Daedalus built
his shrine to Aphrodite.
Concrete tower blocks
obscure the view now
from downtown Trapani.
But up there,
the air is something else –
pine forest-rare,
like Aphrodite's curly hair.

Just minutes
from the sweating streets,
quarried cliffs overshadow
pasturing cows in verdant fields,
grey-leafed olive groves, and the abandoned hotel.
The bus keeps moving the scenery forwards,
but my vision takes in 360 degrees –
I've got eyes in the back of my head.

My ears pop and stomach lurches
as we go higher and higher,
winding up the spiral road,
each bend and roll synchronises
with Mariah Carey's perfectly pitched high notes,
You've got me feeling emotion playing on the radio.

Petrified, we arrive,
happy to be alive.

Erice: we went there twice.
The first time was just as thrilling
swaying in the funivia,
which runs on magnets round and round
aerial pylons like circulating blood.

We are clouds
higher than islands,
higher than clouds.
As magnificent as the views
and part of the world,
not just spectators.

Letting our spirits rise,
we come together
with rocks and trees,
sensing the danger
and the absolute necessity
of the mountain top.

ERICE II

Among the pines
we sit like sprites
on sunlit steps,
prising the lid off
a beer bottle
with a lighter.

I decide
to drink a cupful,
although the air
is working wonders
on my decrepit lungs.

I don't resist the alcohol –
a fine reward,
as if I had walked
all the way up the mountain.

SUGAR

Out of England,
there is no rain,
just the sound
of scooters braking in
narrow passageways.

The baker
lifts his shutters early
tempting us with sugar
throughout the day.

The world stands still for siesta,
frustrating the thirsty traveller,
who just can't keep
to the rhythm of the natives.

Continental European punks
fuelled on espressos and cheap wine,
party until first light,
keeping weary travellers awake.

An Aeolion Island

The hydrofoil is mashing the sea, throwing up undines with
vicious tails. The sun is scorching and no formal welcome
greets us, just the shouts of weather-beaten fishermen
on the dock. The town has prepared for hungry tourists by
hiking up their prices. We eat our plaited pastries sulkily,
paying a euro over the odds for a coffee.

At the lido the sea is playful, but not inviting. We move on
towards Punta Rossa, where the air stiffens and I hear an
insistent muttering on the wind. There is a house with a
high walled garden on the road just before the turning
to the cove.

The muttering gets louder, and suddenly a sun baked hand
pokes out from the oculus set in the solid wooden garden
gate as if groping around for freedom. I am terrified and
delighted all at once by the disembodied hand, whose
mumbling owner is somehow imprisoned on this paradise
island.

Hurrying on, I turn the corner, and gasp. The sea is
alternate pools of turquoise and indigo. I want to
immerse myself in it, but see no other swimmers. I don't
take chances anymore; I'm as vulnerable as everyone else.
So we sit and eat and drink outside, feeding coastal ants
bread crumbs bigger than their own bodies.

Punta Rossa at last! A solitary yacht has dropped anchor
and people are bathing on the rocks. I walk with butterflies
along the well-worn causeway and, jettisoning my shorts
and sandals, I swim through a sea-worn arch reminiscent of
Durdle Door in Dorset. The turquoise patches are the
deepest and I tread water with ease. I am as buoyant and
light as a cork. Curious fishes come to me.

These are the rocks where Odysseus is thought to have
landed when he encountered the Cyclops. I search the caves
and find nobody.

A Solar Priestess

She can't outrun the sun.
Underneath her boat the sea is molten silver,
and a billion stars have fallen into the ocean.

The port of Palermo welcomes her with
a face full of beauty and the grasping arms
of a needy and selfish woman whose
stink lingers on the air, choking you
with blasphemous fumes.
She pulls her trolley over dog shit
while angels direct the traffic:
the city is a stew.

She's going to Agrigento from platform number 5.
A fight breaks out on the concourse
in front of transient witnesses.
The moment passes,
the stink continues.
She looks at the nice people:
the girl with glasses,
the couple with child,
well dressed strangers
off down the line,

where ficas and pampas grass
grows between the tracks.

Palermo is full of old housing and rail yards,
a bit like Kings Cross.
We are quickly away from the city under rocks.

The train is moving inland
to where the earth rises and undulates.
There is fire in the mountains
where the sun illuminates
the cabbage fields and the river beds are dry.
Plough fields are ochre and ringed
with pale green trees in alkaline soils.
The hedgerows riding the palomino hills
mark each burnished mound with a cross.

The sun disappears and there is fire near the tracks,
as a full moon is rising overhead.
She contemplates the moon, it contemplates her.

Only hours earlier she was a solar priestess,
her forehead branded and scorched
on the boat crossing the water from the island.

The hydrofoil couldn't outrun the sun,
no matter how fast it went.
The sun had lit the trail
that ran constant with her journey.

But the train to Agrigento easily outruns the moon,
which waves farewell and falls out of the race,
then catches up, and falls behind again.

The station is deserted when she arrives,
apart from a dad showing his son the train just in.
Her trolley wheels slide over cool marble floors,
she steps out into the warm, dark unknown.

AGRIGENTO

She climbs the ragged streets of Agrigento. The place is a strange medieval city teeming with all different religious denominations and badly dressed clerics lurk on every corner. Up she climbs the cobbled streets pulling on her trolley. She starts to feel like Christ carrying the cross up to the Mount.

People on the street seem to know what they're doing. They sit in little groups calling out to passers-by. '*Want sex?*' a woman's voice hisses from one of the wrought iron balconies, responding to the sound of the trolley wheels.

She wants this journey to be about something new, but finds herself walking nauseatingly back into the past. She reaches Via Duomo, the highest street in Agrigento where the air is better. A pope slept in the Catholic Museum here and they haven't changed the sheets since.

A man looks on smugly when she gets no answer at the B&B Liola. It's disconcerting because she sees her own strained reflection in the mirrored front door. Finally, the door opens. Her room is a yellow temple, a golden tomb.

CHESIL BEACH

I am swimming in the Fleet Lagoon. My fears – conscious, unconscious and imagined – are all amplified by the water. I'm climbing the shimmering steps of the sun's reflection on the cool surface. Cutting my knees on stones, there is blood and salt again.

I hear, so clearly, the conversations of the people in their blackened wooden huts, small settlements on the stony bank across the water. The labradors, playing in the shallows could almost be mistaken for mermaids. I'm listening to the slow, mechanical flap of the cormorant's wings and the swallows skimming between diving seagulls.

Breathing in the heady scent of elderberry flowers, we walked a green corridor of hedgerows down to the lagoon. The path was festooned with red admirals, blackberries and field convolvulus.Three wasps nests, and a horde of sparrows and finches busied there.

The sporadic humans whose paths cross in this oxygenated tunnel are obliged to acknowledge each other with a cheery hello.

Reaching the shore we stopped by the rusty boat that has disintegrated more between each visit. I always run right out to it, getting my feet wet, wondering at the steel flaking to fine russet lace, and touching the traces of paint gleaming cobalt blue like a jay's wing under the sun.

Later that day the coast guard rowed up to us and asked if we had seen a naked man running along the bank. A strange, dark excitement took hold of me thinking that someone had dared to enter such a primal state on this jurassic beach.

Our faces straight, we answered no, but after the coast guard pushed off and the helicopter flew on overhead, laughing out loud, we began to undress.

CHEMISTRY

Is this the last day of summer? I'm scared to go inside in case I miss a moment of sunshine. My days in Aix-en-Provence were all about the air, water, flowers and trees around the Jas de Bouffan, where Cezanne once lived.

There are giant centipedes on the otherwise empty paths around Mont Sainte-Victoire, which rises above swathes of red clay soil and silent vineyards. Plane trees overarch the Rue Nostradamus on the way to Arles, where Vincent's sunflowers are blooming in the fields next to the Langlois Bridge. And the canal teems with old bicycles and weeds, but provides a cool respite from the ferocious heat.

Coming back to England, there is a different kind of warmth, definitely damper, and a cooler, wetter, more acidic green, and I feel that certain sort of melancholy, the one I felt when growing up. A milky sky has obscured the sun and made the morning strange. Now a spider turns her back on her web and scurries under the parsley pot. The boom of an aeroplane pierces the charged atmosphere.

It's that moment before it rains when the nitrogen and oxygen rearrange their atoms, releasing the pungency of trees and birds and catalysing my memories. It all becomes chemistry.

RANDOM
(LIGHT AND MATTER)

Random

People like paper,
light shines
through cubes of sugar.

Time of floating gradients,
monkey dances,
axis spins and man moves
through windows,
shattering the final curtain.

Coins spin: heads or tails?
Money, diamonds, horses, gold?
It's a growing story, isn't it?

Never going to grow old,
or explode.
Spinning like a wheel,
a model,
or a carousel.

It's just me, being weird,
in this house of cards.

BLADDER STONES

The catheter is a silicon needle
opening her narrow urethra:
urine flows
and drip-drips

the crystalline bits
and mucus,
softly spilling over hand held mirror.

She sees herself reflected,
siphoning the stone-forming
sediments of a gifted little sister.

ARIA TO GREED

A fistful of coins
spoiled your face.
It's such a shame
that all that keeps you here is gain.

Why can't you forget money
for a minute?
Is there anything else you want,
something altogether different?

Does it all come down
to what's in your bank account?
Stacking it up to some obscene amount:

What's it all about?

Something material,
not at all ethereal.
Let's get right down to the nitty-gritty,
And count the coins in your kitty.
Money loves money, loves money, loves money.

Homo Luminous

Red shadows
hide under trees,
lurking in the darkness,
taking sanctuary.

But listen,
your name is humming on the summer wind,
your face, an imprint on every leaf.
And the light will find you in the end,
my friend,
the light will find you in the end.

The storm winds are blowing stronger
now mighty Jupiter strides the sky,
and we have been called to revolution,
the shifting time is nigh.
Dionysus has had his way with us,
Apollo has had his day.

And the light will find us all,
my friend,
the light will find us in the end.

RED SAMBUCCA

Red Sambucca's framed
her golden four leaf clovers,
and painted pretty pentagrams
on her garden gate.

She smiles like a concubine
with overflowing goblets of wine,
her molten hands bring on the night,
her amber eyes beg for sunrise.

She believes in the universe,
in the spirit of pure energy,
and the electrified flesh that transmutes
her desire for all creativity.

She walks the woodland pathway
to the fairy tree
and sets a ring
of fire for everyone to see
her intention is strong.

BLACK SAMBUCCA

Who is that woman
shuffling the cards
of Destiny and Fate,
teasing the scorpion
and charming the snake?
She's Black Sambucca.

Who is this? Spinning
and weaving eternal threads,
clapping hands with casternets,
shifting pitch on instruments
she plays so well.
Is it Black Sambucca?

Who is that woman
with feathers and bones,
beads and strings,
sticks and stones,
transported as she sings?
It is Black Sambucca.

LOONY

There
is cackling
laughter when I
lift the receiver. Someone
is ascending the stairs. Armed
with a plastic bottle, I
rush around in
despair.

KINESTHETIC

She's kinesthetic –
learns through touch.

Needs a cuddle,
it's not enough.

Needs more,
she's an addict,
but owns it.

Parades it,

strips it bare
and bones it,
takes it in
and homes it.

Then beats herself up!

A Heavy Squeak

A heavy squeak of a red
telephone box's
door springs.

The clicking sound
of the dial
always running back to zero,
unless it gets stuck.

Money drops
if you're lucky.

Smells echo sound:
Urgent pips and piss
in the corner.

The stale taste of the mouthpiece:
unresolved needs,
anxiety supressed,
anticipating breath
with a cigarette.

POET

A glistening feather made of metal,
something sleek,
a moving shadow.

Ferocious fire-spirit,
sleeping
in a cold cage of her own making.

A shining continuum,
glowing in a frame
of geraniums.

ELEMENTS

WATER

Water has structure,
water has art;
bright ripples
and dark floods.

Water sweeps you up
or drags you down.
Flowing rhythmically,
making sounds:
swirling and bubbling,
its changes profound.

A trickle, then a river
rushing to the patient ocean.
Dissolving my emotions
and salty tears of regret.
Water remembers,
and water forgets.

CRYSTAL WATER

It's water we need now, not the rocks. We want to flow with the roll of the streams and tap the source of this sustainable sun.

But the rocks drag our heads down in despair, knotting our braids and breaking our life bonds.

So take the crystal water from mountain springs and on bone frozen days speak words of love to newborn snowflakes. See them kaleidoscope more intricately than ever before.

Shout out words of hate and see those snowflake crystals mutate.

FIRE

Fire, I am your daughter
and I tended to your flame.
Once I tried to reach you,
but your touch meant only pain.

Your atom dance has many colours,
a swaying hypnotic seduction
consuming all that comes too close
with an appetite for destruction.

Fire, blazing in my face,
you dazzle with energy, spitting with rage,
and I was taught to fear you
at such an early age.

Now I am master of the roaring fire,
stoking up the hissing pyre,
releasing sparks into night skies
dancing about our heads like fireflies.

Rain

I remember rain
as an old friend
come to soften the darkest hour
between night and day,

to cool the sun's infrared,
rinsing down the walls and windows,
flushing out the streets

and clearing space for more pollution.

The staccatto beats of rhythmical rain on
my rooftop are non-stop,
super-fast games of ping pong.

But too much rain unnerves me:
I turn on my inner sun
to erase the blankness of the sky.

MOTHER-AIR (IN ESSENDON)

The mottled and curly-headed
clouds stand still for a second,
and, opening their mouths, they command:
'Connect with your body.'

I get closer to the ground than gravity.

Keep me here
where we can sit around
on luscious lawns
and let the torn air of day
relieve our alcohol stricken heads.

I cut fine slices
of ginger from the root
for us to chew
and re-hydrate.

You two are in my green ambit:
there will be flowers, kind words,
sustenance
and mother-air.

WIND

The wind whirls and hovers like an ogre
blasting out his woes, and my windows shake,
resisting the clatter of his angry blows.

Sunday morning – time to listen to the wind.
You clear your throat and say,
'*Monday is a world away,
and Tuesday hardly matters.*'

But the wind howls out its chilling message.
A police siren catches the wind moaning:
the sounds combine, frequencies overlapping;
long wails and then staccato whooping
in and out in ululation.

His dog barks twice, the front door slams,
the Sunday husband's in a jam.
A bitter wind locks him out,
his wife can't hear his impatient shout.
He shouts again, but is unheard,
the wind will have the final word.

THUNDER MIND

The deluge of never-ending rain on the gazebo
is a wildly enthusiastic round of applause.
and then, boom!
Thunder rolls down the chimney stack into the room
and, seconds later, lightning stripes my eyes.

A voice in my clairaudient ear says:–
'This applause could be for you. Perform!
Why hold back your thunderstorm?
Let the rain dissolve your stagnant thoughts,
and move you downstream,
where you can be heard and seen.'

But soon the insistent rainstorm abates
and the tin-wispy sound
of a train whistle fills the hush.
A patch of blue appears,
the air lightens,
the childrens' cries are heard again.

Thor has blitzed the dirty white sky
and torn a hole in the gutter,
through which raindrops
patter on the plastic roof
as regularly and insistently
as a heartbeat.

SONGS:
LYRICS OF
CHANGE
AND
INTEGRATION

TAKE IT SLOW

I take one day at a time,
take it all in my stride.
I'll always want to be here,
sometimes I want to shine.
Shaking down my long hair,
always one to care.
Never let what's worth having go,
try to take it slow.
What I want is what I give,
the life I have I've got to live.
No-one treats me second best,
grace is here forgive the rest.

Man, oh man, I don't have to rescue,
no cracked walls, I've got a breakthrough.
A lovely mind will always make do,
giving my best to you.
I watch the sunset every night,
seeing the darkness and the light.
I know that fear distorts the mind.
I'm looking out, I'll surely find
someone who wants to be here,
who really needs to care.
Never let what's worth having go,
try to take it slow.

So Long

So long, power patterns,
roses scattered in my bed.
Straight lines, no distractions,
keep the focus in my head.

Don't go parking in my space,
you're way, way out of line.
Don't go taking up my place,
I'm not your fool this time.

Good bye, bad behaviour,
save it for another life.
Spare me your constellation,
leave the orbits of my mind.

Gold rays, sweet vibration,
lift me to a higher plane.
Farewell, strange relation,
made me heal this hurt and shame.

Don't go parking in my space
your way, way out of line.
Don't go taking up my place,
I'm not your fool this time.

SOUL TWIN

Soul twin, falling down,
falling down again.
Am I bad for you,
bad for you, my friend?

You glow like a frosted pearl,
stolen from the sea.
You twirl like a pretty girl,
half as bad as me.

Soul twin, why have you gone
to the thing that makes you cry?
Time to build a life,
a life that lets you fly.

You gleam like a dream machine,
t-cut to the chrome.
You itch like a nervous witch,
I see you're not coming home.

Stop pretending,
they'll be a happy ending,
because baby, I know
that you're sinking.

FEEL THE GRACE

Whatever's in your heart is in mine.
Whatever colours you have lost, I'll find.
Whenever you're listening, I'll sing
you a song that means something.

And when the cold's too much to bear,
suddenly I am standing there.
The tears are frozen on my face,
that's when I feel the grace.

Whatever lies you try, I've tried them too.
Whatever fears you hide, have hidden you.
Whenever we kiss, I'm kissing you.
Whatever your path, be true.

And when the heat's too much to bear,
suddenly I am standing there.
The laughter's creasing up my face,
that's when I feel the grace.

BOOK OF LIFE

Writing all of my life, it helps me through.
Writing all of my life, long lines just for you.
Each word a flying bird.
Each sentence needing to be heard.
Each line a catchy hook,
your chapter's making up my book,
book of life.

Trying all of my life, to see the truth about me.
Crying some of the time, too much feeling guilty.
Each day I'm making hay,
I have to make it my own way.
Each tear a hidden fear,
I'll make it in another year,
book of life.

I'm crying, crying to really feel.
I'm dying, dying to really heal.
Dreaming could make it real.
Dreaming could make it real,
book of life.

Trying all of my life,
just to feel the music,
sliding some of the time,
try not to abuse it.
Each day I'm on the run,
six senses bound up with the sun.
Each page, I make it though,
I'm writing my way home to you,
book of life.

A Female Oscar Wilde

A thousand doorways to a thousand skies,
she'd love to rest her eyes.
Being content would suit her fine,
shadows and light, a bottle of wine.
'I'll never leave you!' he lied.
'I'll never leave you!'she cried,
just like a female Oscar Wilde.

A thousand windows to a thousand skies,
she'd love to be outside
on this Indian summers day,
breeze blowing gently, hearing him say,
'I'll never leave you!' he lied.
'I'll never leave you!' she cried,
like a female Oscar Wilde.

A thousand mornings she awoke to his smiles,
now she has to let him go.
She's asking forgiveness
for what, I don't know.
'I'll never leave you,' he lied,
I'll never leave you,' she sighed,
like a female Oscar Wilde.

THE JUGGLER

She met him on a Sunday, his hair as black as coal,
with his chips and chocolate children,
and his water colour soul.
He said how she reminds him
of his old girlfriend Eileen,
she was doubly delighted to be
his new found queen.

I'll juggle you, he said, take you to my bed,
I'll pull you up, and then I'll let you fall,
heal your heart with beauty, even do your duty,
and then I'll steal the colours of your soul.

She laughed at all his stories,
shared in all his glories,
'til she touched his sorrow and his pain.
She'll help him get behind this,
help him to unwind this,
'til her love can transform them to a flame.

He said this can't work between us:
the wrong Mars and the wrong Venus,
and you know star-crossed lovers
can't change who they are.
So he left her for another,
now she's a single mother,
softly strumming silly love songs on guitar.

Radical Dissident

He's a radical, a dissident,
an outlaw from the Government.
He's magnificent, his hair is wild,
you can see he's nobody's child.

He fixes medicine in the garden,
the long day is forgiven again.
He takes the lantern from his father,
and brings it down the mountain.

There's a place where we were younger,
nights are warm and spirits hunger,
and I could always see your mercy,
your mercy.

I'm an artist, a healer,
I deal in gold and silver.
I'd like to share some time with you,
but baby, I'm just looking through
to another world, another time,
when you were promised to be mine.
Now you're gone and things have changed,
but you will always know my name.

There's a place where we were younger,
nights are warm and spirits hunger,
and I could always see your mercy,
your mercy.

DIVAS

Divas and their beavers wearing suits and ties,
checking out the men who stand in single file.

Waiting to be heard, just waiting to be heard,
outside the dying rooms of patriarchal rule.

Come on woman, live up to your name.
Come on women, leave this town called shame.

Power dressing, red lips ain't the way at all.
Shaving up your armpits and craving over balls.

Giving and receiving like an eco-warrior.
Mother Earth calls you, she's screaming out you name.

You are perfect, you are needed, love on every plane.
Come on woman, live up to your name.

Come on woman, live up to your name.
Come on men, leave this town called shame.

Protest Song

Armies of green angels,
descending through the stems.
We're going to make the right amends,
insults to our crops has got to stop.

GMO constructs, you know they leak into the soil.
Killer organisms are never worth our toil.

We're going to rip them up, tear them out,
dig them up and smash them, trash them,
throw them onto the fire,
throw them onto the fire.

Now they're in the seeds,
spreading by the breeze.
Now all the birds and bees
have a corporation's disease.

Genetic pollution is not a solution,
organic revolution for our future constitution.
Someone's got to speak this language,
Someone's got to stop the damage,
together we can heal,
together we can heal.

The world is not a lab,
we are not the rats.
Humanity – get off the slab!

WILD ANIMALS

We are wild animals,
wouldn't you agree?
Scared curious creatures
coming from the sea.
We're changing our dances
as evolution advances.
We're changing our pulses
with revolutionary trances.

Manmade mankinds,
producing paradigms.
Free wildernesses
within the rails of time.
Nature is roving, she's moving
freely through space-time.
Nature is laughing,
she's the backbone of plans.

We are the forests,
somewhere deep in time,
future fossil fuels,
we're almost out of our mines.
We're roaming for reasons,
patrolled by our seasons,
climatical treason
by the hand of mankind.

FLUFFY CREATURE

You are such a fluffy creature,
I would love to make you mine.
Will you be my double feature,
until the end of time?

You are such a funky lover,
I would love to make you mine.
Will you be my softest cover,
until the end of time?

The story goes, our love, it grows,
blow up my nose, tread on my toes.

You are such a fluffy creature,
I would love to make you mine.
Will you be my bestest teacher
until the end of time?

The story goes, our love, it knows,
blow up my nose, tread on my toes.

Sweetness

Sweetness, put the day to rest.
Sweetness, I am really blessed
by your nearness, your clearness,
making me strong.

Sweetness, it's pretty clear to see
you're getting through to me
with spirit and energy.
I'm seeing green and blue,
I am split in two,
Sweetness.

Don't leave, don't run away,
you can stay another day.
Sweet talking me, what can I do?
I am split in two.

Sweetness, it's pretty clear to hear
that you've been rhyming,
your clever melodies,
your timing!
The poets got a muse.
What am I to choose?
Sweetness.

LAZY DAY

I spent a lazy day in bed
because I felt so broken hearted.
It was raining in my head,
the city cold, your love departed.

I played a game of solitaire,
to save myself from my despair.
But, as I let you slip away,
familiar feelings inside me stay.

My friends came round to comfort me,
we found some peace under the duvet.
We laughed away the whole long day,
and ordered junk food takeaway.

You will always hear me say,
I'm going to love you anyway,
because I can change the way I feel,
losing your love was no big deal.

JUST BE FRIENDS

I'm waiting, all alone,
contemplating these times.
Trying to own the way I really feel.
We'll just be friends, this time.

You're my river,
I am what you lost,
somewhere down the line.
You're heart is broken,
so bring it close to mine.
We'll just be friends, this time.

I'm open, hearing your call,
blue confusion sounds so good.
I know that I can't go out with you,
you know I never could.

You're my river,
I am what you lost,
somewhere down the line.
You're my treasure,
I'm the ruby in the dust.
We'll just be friends, this time.

BODY BROKEN

My body's broken, washed up on the shore.
My heart's a token of what it was before.

Am I still bleeding? Sometimes it's hard to tell.
Am I still breathing? The heaven of your hell.

My style's forlorn now, can't even stand up straight.
The weight of sorrow was laid upon my fate.

Am I still grieving, how it used to be?
When you were breathing your life right into me.

I remember riding on the underground of fame
I remember what you told me in the game:

'Surrender to the fire of the flame,
Reach into the light, we're all the same.'

SAILOR

Do not pity me,
for I am a sailor.
You cannot overwhelm me,
because I've already won.

I've already won
the silly games you're playing.
You cannot overwhelm me,
because I've already won.

We all need to live.
I served my time,
and lord knows
you've been loved
and lord knows
I've been loved.

Two Hands Strong

What is real is surreal,
what is right is wrong.
When cracks appear in reality,
we must be two hands strong.

When life is keenly shifting
between trouble and desire
and control seeks to blind us
we must be two hands strong.

I still believe in revolution.
I still believe in change,
and burn my fires on water
reflecting on my rage.

One hand might be shaking
while the other beats the drum.
When all around is crumbling,
we must be two hands strong.

A Reflection - Minute Particles

I focus on my punishments
instead of my abundance.
Revisiting the old palaces of pain:
rolling out the fear, the loss,
letting myself make a fuss.

I grieve awhile and move on again.
My minute particles expanding like bubbles.
Particles of me, particles of you,
a collision of beautiful truth.

Is this the real life or just the ride?
Life is bestowed,
Atma, self-unified.
All is one, one is all.

I was right all along
to hold on.

SPIRIT

The SUN is
central to this light
and is the guiding star
of our SHIFT. Connecting
us with the Great Central SUN is
DIVINE LOVE, the source of all truth,
the fiery realm of pure spirit and energy. A
spiral arm galaxy holds the centre point of creation,
a cosmic storybook with ANCIENT and eternal ROOTS.
Spirit maintains the stars and creates spirit, and vice-versa.

For Cassidy

Thanks to my editor Nick Papadimitriou,
for his unfailing commitment to seeing *Garland*
through to the stage that it is at now.

Thanks also to Jay Ramsay, whose editorial
skills and stylistic suggestions galvanised me
into getting *Garland* together as a collection.
See http://www.jayramsay.co.uk/

Thanks to Andrew Watton for production. And to
Fiona Burcher-Jones, general muse, sub-editor
and proof-reader.